About The Author

Susan Camille Bauman-Jorgensen
July 11, 1961-January 4, 1993

Susan was born in St. Louis, Missouri in, 1961. The family moved to Caldwell, Idaho when Susan was three years old.

As a preschooler, Susan began to study ballet and violin. As a result of the loving relationships shared between Susan and her instructors, June Itami and Walter Cervany, music became a major and abiding passion in her life.

While in high school, in the Caldwell area, she enjoyed participating in a Madrigal singing group and a theatre production of "Fiddler on the Roof" where she donned top-hat, tails and mustache to play the "fiddler."

Susan began her college experience at Boise State University under a music scholarship. A sophomore exchange took Susan to Rutgers University where she found it only a short train ride to New York City and the theatre. She also became involved in Lutheran Campus Ministry, traveling to Washington D.C. for interviews with members of Iranian hostages at the American Embassy following the Reagan Inauguration. In 1983, she returned to Boise State University where she began studying psychology and playing with the Boise Philharmonic Orchestra.

The following year Susan was off to Matsumoto, Japan where she spent a year and received certification as a Suzuki Violin Educator from Dr. Shinichi Suzuki.

After graduating from the College of Idaho in 1985 Susan moved to the Boston area where she soon began her nearly six year association with McLean Psychiatric Hospital, a Harvard University teaching and research facility.

It was here that she met Paul Jorgensen. They were married on July 7, 1989 in Bonners Ferry, Idaho, her parents' home town.

Susan had recently completed work as a research assistant collaborating on papers dealing with obsessive compulsive disorders and depression. Sue and Paul also ran a residential treatment facility in Newton Centre, living with and counseling residents with disabling psychiatric illnesses. In addition Susan had resumed part-time Suzuki teaching. It was in the summer of 1992 when she became a full-time instructor at The Suzuki School of Newton, The School of Creative Arts/Reading and The Winchester Community Music Schools.

Susan loved to travel and visit her many international friends; enjoying a Christmas in London and a New Year's in Edinburgh. Another Christmas was spent in Japan introducing her Buddhist friends to Santa Claus in her tiny apartment.

Blessed with such enthusiasm for life, Susan is best remembered for her generous and loving nature and constant efforts to gather her friends and family about her and to express her affection with wit and good humor.

In Search Of The Japanese Spirit in Talent Education

A Research Essay

By Susan C. Bauman

Design: Aean Pinheiro

ISBN-10: 0-87487-767-9
ISBN-13: 978-0-87487-767-0

INTRODUCTION

What is Talent Education? In the United States, Talent Education is commonly referred to as the "Suzuki Method," after its creator and founder Shinichi Suzuki. Suzuki has said many times in his lessons to teachers, "Study is change, I change myself - this is study." Masami Kojima, a writer for the *Mainichi Shimbun* Japanese daily, and recent author of *The Revolution of the World's Children* sums up Talent Education in this way: "In order for the student to change, the teacher must change" (Kojima, 2). The concept of change which these men are alluding to can be better understood if we look at the usage of the word "change" in Japanese. The Japanese verb *kawaru* is commonly used to denote continual change as opposed to an abrupt occurrence (Corwin, 43). It is from the Japanese root word *kau* (to buy) that the word *kawaru* (to change) comes. The ideal is for the teacher to study himself, and change himself continually in order to be successful in teaching children, and the goal of Talent Education is to teach the child to change himself, to study himself, to "buy" something for himself.

Before I went to Japan to study Talent Education, I defined the Suzuki Method as a method of teaching young children how to play the violin (or piano, cello, flute, viola or harp). After only a year of study, however, the meaning of Talent Education not only changed for me but somehow began to escape definition. The factors contributing to this change are the result of my encounter with Japanese thought on many levels. There was the cultural experience itself, including such factors as societal differences, my relationships with Japanese students and friends, and the study of the Japanese language, and then, the whole approach to Talent Education in Matsumoto, Japan, including insight into the man, Suzuki, as well as into the influences which inspired him and his philosophy.

These influences underlie the reason I find Talent Education difficult to define in Western terms. However, I think Talent Education can best be seen as two separate but interdependent educational ideals:

1) a philosophy of education embedded in Japanese culture, a philosophy whose goal is to create "noble human beings"; and

2) a philosophy of education which uses the mother-tongue approach, an approach which holds that children can learn anything at an early age if it is taught in the same manner as their native language.

At the Sixth International Conference of Talent Education, Suzuki reiterated words he has spoken many times: "As quickly and easily as children learn their native language, they can learn music and other areas of study without toil." But he was also very quick to add, "Our activities are not directed at producing professional musicians, but persons of beautiful sense - outstanding human beings." The first statement is the method, and the second is the philosophy. Both are equally important in fulfilling his ultimate goal - to have an impact on the world by promoting world peace through education. Suzuki believes that this goal can be achieved when the world's children are nurtured through education by way of the mother-tongue method, thereby creating good human beings. He insists that if the world is to change, it must begin by training the character of children. In a speech given at the United Nations Suzuki said:

> "I have often pondered whether or not if all nations and races were to concern themselves more with this type of education, a much better atmosphere of understanding and peace among men might be the end product" (Suzuki, 1973, 12).

In the West, the method and the philosophy are not seen as interdependent ideals. For example, I have heard many descriptions of the Suzuki Method in the United States, ranging from "a method of playing the violin by ear," to "a method of group instruction," and even "a method of producing young child prodigies." These descriptions only reinforce my contention that in the United States at least parents and even some teachers are more concerned with the "method" than with the "philosophy." They seem to be looking for the external attributes of the method in children, such as quick progression from one piece of music to another, rather than the internal progression of changes in a child's heart and character. In fact, many parents and teachers in the United States cause their children to dislike their instrument and quit playing as a result of continual forcing. Suzuki has warned that "to force the curriculum is to produce the drop-out" (Suzuki, 1973, 9).

So how does one teach a three-year old something as difficult as the violin? Suzuki would say, "Without teaching," because he equates teaching with forcing, something he pointed out in a speech given at the Japan Institute of Educational Psychology:

> In Japanese the word for education is *kyoiku. Kyo* means "to teach," and *iku* means "to bring up." There is considerable subtlety here when we become aware that "teaching" produces drop-outs and "bringing up" produces well-balanced children, and that the two combine to make a child's ability his very own (Suzuki, 1973, 9).

In other words it is the parent and the teacher who guide the child, but it is the child who is actually "teaching" himself. If the child senses that he is being taught or forced, he will give up. Thus, it is a goal of Talent Education to make a child's ability "his own" by giving him an environment in which he can develop his character to its full potential, regardless of how he plays the instrument.

This goal can be better understood by Westerners if we understand that the words "talent" and "ability" are synonymous in the Japanese language. Furthermore, the Japanese word *saino* has a broad meaning by Western standards; not only does the word mean "talent" or "ability," it is also used to denote personality traits. For example, one can create the talent/ability to become a musician just as one can create the talent/ability to become a good person (Suzuki, 1981, 1). And in Talent

Education these two qualities are essential if one is to be called "a good musician."

> When we observe how character is formed, we see that it too, is a talent: it is formed through the adaptation of natural sources of ability to the environment. There may be hereditary elements to this thing called character. . .however I would like to discuss character in the intellectual and spiritual senses. Even then such factors as hereditary differences in physical strength and inner organs influence spiritual development, but these, I think, should be handled as conditions for formation of character rather than character itself (Suzuki, 1984, 29).

In contrast to the Japanese view of *saino,* English has separate definitions for "ability" and "talent". We tend to define ability as one's genetic potential, modified by his environmental conditions. If we say that Jack is not realizing his potential in school, we are actually saying that he has the ability to do the work, but some environmental or personal problem is interfering with his work. The English word "talent" on the other hand, has its roots in the Latin word talenta - (money or a unit of weight) and has evolved into a word meaning "one's God-given, predestined abilities." For this reason the word is generally reserved for referring to the highly artistic, creative individual.

For instance, when a person says, "I used to play the piano, but I quit because I had no talent" he is actually saying, "I have the ability, but no talent." Rarely does a Westerner think of "creating" talent in the same way as "creating" ability. In the West you must have "talent" to justify playing the piano; but in Japan, ability and talent are synonymous, there is no distinction. Therefore developing the ability for mathematics is like developing the ability to play baseball or to play the flute. Furthermore, these talents are not considered as separate entities, but as part of one's overall character. In Japan, if a person has worked at creating his ability to play baseball and he is good enough to play in the big leagues, it is not expected that he will continue if he would rather be a mathematician. The expectation in the West tends to be different. Since talent is considered to be God-given and predestined, not only must we continue in baseball if we have the talent, but we are expected to discontinue playing the piano if we have "no talent."

Upon my arrival in Matsumoto it was pointed out to me that a high percentage of the students who had studied music at the Talent Education Institute from age three or four had actually quit their lessons by the age of fourteen. I was shocked to learn this because most of the fourteen-year-olds, and in fact most of the Japanese students over ten years of age, were at my level of ability or well beyond it. I thought about how children of their "talent" in the Western sense would not be allowed to quit in the United States after such miraculous accomplishments. It was mind-boggling to think that Suzuki was producing child prodigies. How could he be happy about producing talented children and drop-outs at the same time? It was a paradox. Yet he was happy, he continually boasted about the fact that only five percent of the Talent Education children go on to be professional musicians. I couldn't see what he saw in the children until my Western mindset had been broken. Because I was looking at the external production of the children, I couldn't see the internal character changes which were taking place. This character development is the purpose of Talent Education in Japan.

The idea of character development through early education and education in the arts is not new to Japan. Suzuki has been highly influenced by an Eastern culture which values character training not only for the good of the individual but for the good of the whole society. These Eastern ideals then are inherent within Talent Education method and philosophy and are often the reason for the criticism of the Suzuki Method in Western countries. The Suzuki Method, I believe is misunderstood and misrepresented in the United States by those teachers who don't understand the underpinnings of Eastern philosophy inherent in the method they propose to teach. In addition, many parents don't understand the original goals of the method as they exist in Japan. This booklet is an attempt to clarify these misunderstandings.

Because Talent Education cannot be abstracted from its cultural roots, I propose to dive into several aspects of the cultural consciousness in Japan, including the system of values and obligations in Japanese society, and the profound role of the Japanese language in cultural cognition. Beyond the cultural consciousness is the similarity of the role of Zen Buddhism in the traditional Japanese arts to its influence on the Talent Education philosophy, including the roles of the master and student. Also of influence are the Japanese historical educational assumptions, including the role of the mother in the education of the young. Suzuki has taken advantage of a culture that has a strong historical emphasis on character training and early education, and has combined the two into a system of education so Eastern that its true intent still remains elusive to the West. It is important then to understand as much about his personal history as possible if we are to see both sides of the criticism the Suzuki Method has received since its acceptance in Western countries.

These facets of Talent Education are most important if we are to comprehend the philosophy and method as intended. My insight into Japanese culture is derived from many sources, and because of limits of time and subjective experience, it remains one of confusion. Confusion as to how I can relate to Western minds the ideals and concepts of Talent Education as they exist in Japan. The English language and the Western mindset leave me very few outlets for describing a philosophy of education which is vague and subtle. Therefore I've found it difficult to relate my experiences without the aid of research. On the other hand, there are undeniably sections of this work that rely solely upon my own interpretations and personal experiences.

The Cultural Consciousness

Is the Spirit of Japan triangular?
Is it, do you think a square?
Why no indeed!
As the words themselves
Explicitly declare,
It's an airy, fairy, spiritual thing
And things that close to God
Can't be defined in a formula
Or measured with a measuring-rod.
(Soseki, 194)

A *gaijin* (foreigner) in search of the Japanese "spirit" experiences an overwhelming desire to grasp something tangible and full of meaning that will once and for all lay to rest the mystery and vagueness that is Japan. But alas, there is no black and white, and no amount of looking, listening, verbalizing can possibly penetrate the elusive quality of the gray. However, there are some concepts in the mind of Japan that offer some insight into that "spirit" - a spirit which is both conscious and unconscious by Western standards, with the two being not totally at odds. The "spirit" encompasses both the conscious and the unconscious in a kind of cultural consciousness.

The cultural consciousness exists through these two distinct areas of cognition. The first is evident through the conceptual ideals of Japanese society as seen through certain values and obligations. These ideals constitute a social identity or reality. The second area of cognition exists through the Japanese language, a language which has essentially three aspects: the written, which is descriptive and provides clear meaning; the spoken, which is ritualistic and subtle; and the non-verbal, which is both ritualistic and intuitive. These two areas combined result in profound effects on the Japanese personal and social identity as well as some actual physical effects on cognition.

The Cultural Conscious

Ideal values in Japan are those which allow meaning to appear through the silent bonds of man and nature, man and man, and man and *kami* (God). The national religion in Japan is Shinto. Because it is of Japanese origin, it managed to survive the influence of Buddhism. Nonetheless, Shinto (literally; the way of the Gods) is characterized by the worship of *kami* which are either mythological ancestors, or phenomena of nature. As Reischauer points out in his book The Japanese: "The line between man and nature was not drawn sharply and unusual or awesome men were easily made into deities" (Reischauer, 42). Also, there exist in the Shinto philosophy *inochi* or deities of nature, which are the life force of man, it is the *inochi* which bind man to *kami* (Shapiro, 67).

It is through nature that man becomes one with *kami;* the three are linked because "Shinto assumes that the earth as given is finally good." In contrast, the traditional Judeo-Christian view is that man is at odds with nature; nature is "the tempter" (Cleaver, 61). Shinto sees man as a part of nature, nature is not something to be conquered, or something inhabited by Satan, the heathen, or even witches; nature includes man, and together they are a part of *kami.* In the Western view of nature, man and God is somewhat different:

> "Man is against God, Nature is against God, and Man and Nature are against each other. . .The human body, which is a mixture of God and Nature, becomes a most bloody fighting arena for these two forces" (D.T. Suzuki, 1956, 232).

Even Ralph Waldo Emerson, an avid reader of Oriental philosophy saw nature as separate from man when he said that "philosophically considered, the universe is composed of Nature and the Soul. . .all that is "Not Me" (art and nature) is Nature" (Cleaver, 61, 1976). So whereas the *inochi* link the Japanese spirit to the *kami,* there exists no relation between Emerson's "soul" and nature - they are distinct and opposite:

> "The dichotomy of Nature and man implies hostility even utter irreconcilability, and is therefore, mutually destructive. . .to the western mind Nature and Man are separate" (D.T. Suzuki, 1959, 133).

If one looks at a Japanese garden, to the shape and obvious hand of man which has been there, he realizes the extent to which the Japanese feel at one with nature. Nature needs man to be complete. The house too is part of nature, made of wood and straw and rice paper; man harmonizes parts of nature into a world which he finds good from the outset. In this way Cleaver suggests that the body, which includes the spirit, becomes one with its surroundings. Comparatively, Americans feel their bodies to be separate from the world, like Emerson.

Another contrast which implies a different cultural mindset is the Japanese view that human beings are essentially good. They are not born as sinners who need "purification" through baptism, but are perfectly acceptable as is. In fact, if a Japanese person should act in an anti-social way, then he is labeled as *hito de nashi* (not human). And a reformed criminal "becomes human once more" (*ma ningen ni kaeru*) (Wagatsuma, 372). The principles which began in Shinto now have formed a kind of consciousness in Japanese society which sees value in the goodness of the world and all that exists within it.

In Japanese *ki* is a word used to describe one' s emotion, consciousness, will, or character. For example if a person becomes mentally ill, one will say *ki ga chigau* - his *ki* has become different (Wagatsuma, 371). Doi has pointed out that in Japan one's *ki* (the spirit of a person) is sometimes not really "himself"; at these times a man becomes his "other self" or controlled by a *mushi* (an insect or bug) (Doi, 1973b, 181). For example, if a man dislikes someone, he says it is his *ki* which is doing the disliking, his *ki* is out of control. Not a good state for one's *ki*. To be depressed also involves being *mushi mi tsukareru*, or "possessed by the bug." In all these instances, the person is a victim of the terrible "insect" (Wagatsuma, 372).

When *mushi* interfere with one's good nature, it creates a state which might make a child throw a tantrum, known as *kan no mushi*. The child was not upset - but the "bug" had once again interfered with the child's *ki*, thus causing bad behavior (Wagatsuma, 372). In fact, traditionally there where Shinto shrines with deities called *mushi kiri* (the "cut off bug") where a distraught mother could go with the hope that she might "cut off" the bug from her child now and then. Otherwise the mother just had to wait until the child became old enough to have his *ki* trained in the marital arts, traditional arts, or Zen (Doi, 1973b, 184).

If a child happens to grow up without proper training in the traditional arts or Zen, he - or rather his *ki mushi*, can become disruptive to society, through inter-personal relationships and such. This person, or rather his *mushi*, must be "cut off" from society by those he comes in contact with. When his *ki* is back to "normal", he is welcomed back into the group.

Unlike in the Judeo-Christian religions, the philosophical influences of Shinto and Buddhism do not impose any ethical or moral codes on Japanese society:

> "There were no ethical concepts associated with these religious ideas, except for a sense of awe and reverence before nature. . ."
> (Reischauer, 42)

Without a code such as the Ten Commandments in the Old Testament, it was up to Japanese society to take on the role of God. The society has accomplished this not by overt rules and regulations, but by patterns of communication required by all individuals who want to maintain their status in the group:

> "Violent confrontation between individuals is restrained not so much by a universal sense of morality. . .as by a system of etiquette more rigid than anything seen in the contemporary Western world" (Buruma, 12).

In contrast, the moral identity existent within the United States is a personality of bi-polar character, as Erik Erikson has pointed out:

> The American, on the whole lives with two sets of principles or religiously pronounced political principles of a highly puritan quality, and

> a set of shifting slogans which indicate what at a given time, one may get away with one the basis of not more than a hunch, a mood, or a notion (Erikson, 1950, 278).

Insight into this major cultural difference can be seen by examining the Japanese concept of *wa* (to harmonize two opposing forces). *Wa* is an ethical concept whose ideal is to integrate individuals for the harmony and balance of the group; often this is at the expense of individual achievement. Rewards are almost always given to the group as a whole, not to individuals who exhibit high accomplishments (Nakane, 52). But for the most part this is acceptable to the Japanese because they believe that individuals cannot achieve without being part of a group.

Traditionally, *wa* has been seen as the uniting of two opposing forces; this concept was adopted by the Japanese from Confucian philosophy (Nakamura, 1967, 146). Also involved is the Buddhist belief that there are no opposites. Eastern philosophy has always appreciated the fine line between opposites, even the possibility that opposites may actually be nonexistent. According to Yukawa Hideki, a Nobel Prize-winning physicist in Japan:

> One of the most fundamental differences between East and West is that the Western mind emphasizes the dualistic aspect of reality while the Eastern mind basically is advaitist. . .Reality (to the Japanese) is non-dualistic. It is not-two, which is not the same as one. It is both yes and no, yet it is neither the one nor the other (Cleaver, 61).

His thinking is based on the Zen concept of one-mind, or the concept that there are no opposites, because there is only one true mind. The Buddha-mind is entered into only when one becomes enlightened through one's own spiritual effort, but Buddha-mind can be discovered in one's own mind because truth is not opposed to reality, but reality exists in truth (Hanayama, 42-43).

There are numerous examples of harmonizing opposites in the Japanese arts, a familiar form of haiku called *Toriwase* (togetherness), written by Yosa Buson (1716-1783), shows that seemingly opposed things can be seen as reliant on one another, and therefore as part of one another:

Tsurigane ni	Alighting on the temple bell
Tomarite nemuru	It sleeps
Kocho kana	A butterfly
(Behn, 23)	

In the Kabuki theatre as well, the audience and actors are brought together by a *hanamichi* (flower pathway), which is an entrance/exit for the actors. The pathway goes directly through the center of the audience, symbolically uniting the active participants with the passive participants, both of whom are of importance to the success of the drama. The *hanamichi* makes it difficult to draw the line between the active and passive participants; in fact, it seems both audience and actor are active in their respective roles, thus harmony has been created out of potentially opposing elements. (D.T. Suzuki, 1959, 297).

Preservation of the *wa* is of value to the individual as well as to society, and, as Wagatsuma points out, may actually be the reason for the ambiguity that the Japanese seem to express, as well as the tolerance which the Japanese seem to have for ambiguous, illogical situations. In the Japanese mind there are positive and negative sides to most situations; the individual remains unruffled by what is clearly unharmonious to the Western mind. Furthermore, this tolerance is seen as a mark of a truly socialized individual:

> "The tolerance of ambiguity and ambivalence in social relations is valued as a sign of one's maturity and character development" (Wagatsuma, 378).

Wa replaces individual freedom of action, but it ensures a group identity. Dore has called "corporatism", the notion in Japan that although he cooperates with the group goals, the individual finds satisfaction in this by ensuring his own welfare, and that therefore the group gives him his autonomy (Dore, 1961, 103). But, as Nakane points out, there are limits:

> "The limits of individual freedom of action are fixed in such a way as to ensure that the activity of the individual will not breach group limits" (Nakane, 86).

It must be pointed out that identity in Japan lies in the group not because the Japanese see the group as more important than the individual, but because the individuals is seen as fused into the group. The group and the individual are not at odds as they may be in the United States; the two are in harmony because they can't exist without each other. In Western society, if the group is given priority over the individuals - the individuals are thought to be "oppressed." This is not the assumption in the Japanese consciousness (Wagatsuma, 374). The differences in identity can be summed up as follows:

> "When asked about his occupation an American will mention that he is an engineer, sociologist, a secretary, while a Japanese will mention who he works for, I work for SONY; I teach at UCLA" (Nakane, 97).

Japanese individuals are cognizant of cultural demands, and even have feeling of frustration about these demands, referred to in Japanese as *honne*; but whereas Americans would speak their feelings and perhaps do something about their state of "oppression", the Japanese are willing to allow their personality to remain a group personality. They will not show their *honne* except in indirect conversation (i.e., nonverbal conversation), or in polls where they can be anonymous (Wagatsuma, 376).

An international poll was taken in 1984 of young people (ages eighteen to twenty-four), in eleven countries, including the United States, Japan, Britain, West Germany, Switzerland, Sweden, Yugoslavia, South Korea, Brazil, and the Philippines. The results, which were published in the Japan Times are is good evidence that *honne* is very much alive in Japanese youth. One of the questions in the poll asked "Do you want to live a life useful to your society?" Only four percent of Japanese youth answered "yes" to that question, the lowest percentage of all the countries polled ("Survey," 15). They were obviously displaying their *honne*, because most likely they will end up being useful to their society. In addition, another forty-nine percent of Japanese youths said they were dissatisfied with the society they lived in - the third lowest in the poll (only France and Brazil were lower). The reason most often stated for their dissatisfaction was the feeling that society would not accept what they thought was just or correct. However, when asked what action they would take to change society, forty-one percent said they would do nothing except go to the polls and vote, twenty-one percent said they would take positive action within the limits of the laws, and only three percent said they would take illegal action ("Survey", 15).

In contrast to *honne* are *tatemae*, opinions that a person will state directly in conversations. *Tatemae* are what maintains the *wa* in society, but both kinds of expressions are "truth" for the individual - that is, they are not at odds. When a person states something about society, he expresses the commitment he feels toward the norms, this is truth. When he admits to himself the frustration he feels about those norms, this is truth also (Doi, 1973b, 183). Thus, the cultural personality lives through the cultural assumption that "life is too complicated for one to make a simple black and white judgement" (Wagatsuma, 377).

So the group identity persists and is possibly to blame for the "identity crisis" that exists in Japan. The search for self-identity has manifested itself in a "national identity crisis." Japanese literature since ancient times has been characterized by this search, but current books called *nihonjin-ron* (the debate about the Japanese) overflow the bookstores in Japan (Reischauer, 148-150). Because the Japanese brought in so many outside influences, like Chinese writing, culture, art, and even written language early in their civilization, the Japanese began wondering "who they were" a long time ago. However the influence from Western countries in the last one hundred years has magnified the crisis into a full-scale debate the Japanese have among themselves. That is why they like to read books about what other people think of them.

The "other people" are those outside of Japan - the foreigners, non-Japanese, or *gaijin*, which in Japanese literally means "outside person." The meaning of *gai* is "outside", and its synonym, is not "inside," but *uchi* which means "house." *Uchi-no* refers to one's own people and *uchi-dewa* to one's place of work or department thereof (Nakane, 125). Depending on the context, *uchi-no* can mean one's family, one's business associates, or one's fellow citizens, but in any context what is implied is an isolated system of people working for the good of the group. A *gaijin* can come inside an *uchi* system, but cannot become a part of an *uchi* unless he has had similar experiences constituting psychological or emotional ties to other members of the *uchi.*

The solidarity and isolation elements of *uchi* are just as important in maintaining the *wa* in Japan as are the separation of *tatemae* and *honne.* And as Wagatsuma points out, they can be just as binding:

> So strong is the distinction between inside and out that while Japanese would never dream of throwing a tattered doll into a garbage can, they remained remarkably indifferent to the plight of millions of miserable refugees drifting on the South China Sea (Wagatsuma, 375).

The isolation of the *uchi* (in this case, the country) overrides any feelings the Japanese might have for doing something about "the plight of millions." The solidarity of the *uchi* can be seen through the emotional tie one has to an inanimate object which is nonetheless a part of the *uchi.*

In the construction of houses, too, one can see both isolation and solidarity. Often there are fences around the house; and even though the houses traditionally are small (only one or two rooms), there are partitions made out of wood and rice paper, giving a mere illusion of privacy within the house itself. The family, like the country, is both isolated from the outside and solidified on the inside. This is a *wa* - preserving device in Japanese culture.

The traditional values of preserving the *wa* in Japan automatically require obligations by individuals, because a group-oriented society creates group-oriented individuals who perpetuate the circle (Benedict, 46). These obligations quite easily begin with human relationships found in the various forms of *uchi,* starting with the unique Japanese concept of *amae.*

The noun *amae* denotes an action of intimacy found in Japanese interpersonal relationships. The word itself has no English equivalent, something Takeo Doi (a Japanese psychologist) finds amazing: "Why, even a puppy does it" (Doi, 1973a, 15). *Amae* refers to one's need for passive love; but it is through the verb forms *amaeru,* to indulge oneself in another's love," and *amayakasu,* "to defer one's love to another person," that the word becomes active (Kumagai, 249).

The aggressive role, *amaeru,* involves a need to be totally indulged in someone else's love or sympathy, without giving anything in return. The passive role, *amayakasu,* requires a kind of "ego-suspension," which will allow the indulgences of another without hesitation - altruistically - thereby conceding one's needs to be loved for the moment (Kumgai, 250).

There are, according to Kumagai, three levels of *amae* within Japanese society: (1) The parent-child pattern, where the parent allows the child's indulgence; (2) The intimate pattern which occurs in personal relationships that are familial or non-familial; this interaction allows either party to be the aggressor; (3) The formal pattern which occurs in societal relationships, but is controlled by ritualized language (Kumagai, 252).

Kumagai points out the importance of the parent-child *amae* relationship in these translated Japanese phrases:

> *"A parent's amae runs deep."*
> *"She did not amayakasu her daughter enough as a child."*
> *"A parent must allow her child to amaeru now and then."*
> *"Without amae, a child will grow up to be defiant."*
> (Kumagai, 258)

Another example from Kumagai shows the pattern of interaction characteristic of *amae* behavior:

> Ichiro is said to amaeru (to indulge himself in amae) when he feigns illness to escape his chores. Mrs. Yamada, his mother, is said to amayakasu (to defer to Ichiro out of permissive love) when she permits his indulgence (in amae) and releases him from his work. She accepts his behavior with an affectionate comment, "My, he's amaeru-ing again. What a child!" (Kumagai, 253)

The interpreting aspect of *amae* behavior between the mother and the child is the child's role as the aggressor. The child in the West who exhibits this kind of behavior is not met with passivity on the part of the mother, but with more aggression, so it becomes a battle between them. This is why Western patterns of mother-child relationships are usually just the opposite: the mother most often has the role of the aggressor, while the child has the passive role (Doi, 1973a, 42).

The parent-child pattern of *amae* can be seen as the pattern which teaches the child a pattern of interaction which he will use the rest of his life, only he will be expected to be able to "defer" in *amae* as well. He begins to *amayakasu* with his siblings and even with his parents, then he begins to *amaeru* and *amayakasu* in social relationships. At this point *amae* takes on an added meaning: reciprocal obligation.

In the social context, the concept of *amae* assumes that both person A and person B require a certain amount of dependency. But before a dependency relationship can take place they must feel a certain amount of intimacy, and until this occurs they exude *enryo* (reserve) at the expense of their *amae* needs. Therefore, in social relationships, person A must not just presume *amae* behavior, but must limit it until person B shows that he wants to provide his nurturance (Doi, 1973l, 96). *Enryo* then becomes a control for *amae* behavior, since it is assumed that all Japanese desire *amae* behavior (Wagatsuma, 374).

Once a pattern for *amae* behavior is established for the individual socially, he is obliged to continue in that relationship. In fact, social relationships are characterized by *amae* interdependence among members of the same *uchi* or group. These relationships are encouraged by the group to bring about solid socialization. Characteristically there is a term to describe a person whose needs of *amae* have been socialized completely; that term is *sunao-na* (Doi, 1973a, 154). Someone who is thought to be *sunao-na* is a person who will not upset the *wa*; thus the whole structure of *amae* in Japanese society contributes to the harmony of the group (Wagatsuma, 373). It is interesting to note that Doi has written much about this socialization process and believes that most of the culture's psycho-neuroses stem from improper, or inadequate *amae* relationships (Doi, 1973a).

If we understand the concept of *amae* as reciprocal obligation, then we can understand how the concept of *on* was born out of that obligatory relationship. *On* can be translated as "indebtedness to others", this entails both obedience and respect in familial relations as well as societal relations (Befu, 54). *On* relationships are always hierarchical and begin of course with the parent-child relationship (Befu, 167-168). Because the parents socialize and nurture the child, the child in return is obligated to the parents. He shows this obligation by displaying *oya-koko* (filial piety) toward his parents, thus repaying the "debt." However, this debt is never fully paid off.

The obligation of *on* is not relinquished even when one would have seemingly given continual service. As Benedict points out, even when one has given a life time of service it only amounts to "returning of one-ten thousandth of one's debt" (Benedict, 83). This phrase was used in the feudal period by samurai who realized the magnitude of their debt to their Lords.

When the *on* obligation is transferred from the parental relationship to the social relationship, it is similar to *amae*. When two individuals become dependent upon one another in the social context, they are bonded to each other through *chu* (loyalty) - a concept which grew out of one's bond or loyalty to the nation or the emperor (Befu, 168). Nakane alludes to the extension of the *oya-koko* relationship as being identical to the principle guiding the structure of Japanese organization in "every kind of institution in Japan" (Nakane, 99-100).

But one does not have built-in societal obligations without having some negative feelings about them. Similar to *honne* in the value system of *wa* is *ninjo* in relation to the *on* debt. *Ninjo* can be defined as one's personal feelings or frustrations about society's requirement of *on.* For example, when only sixteen percent of Japanese youths polled said that they would work for the country's interests at the expense of their own, they were displaying their *ninjo* about the strict system of loyalty required by individuals in Japan ("Survey," 15). But *ninjo* has no bearing on what they actually do; interestingly enough *ninjo* is the

> "facet which allows a man who contributes little (to society), to remain in the group, comfortably keeping his status so long as he remains loyal and does not run counter to group activity" (Nakane, 86).

Opposing one's *ninjo* is the concept of *giri,* which is defined as not only one's social obligation, but one's ethical obligation as well. *Giri* is what controls one's *ninjo.* The source of *giri* and its subsequent permanence in Japanese society is the feudalistic chivalry called Bushido (the way of the samurai) (Nitobe, 3). Buruma says that

"The *giri* of the loyal retainers is not based on logic or reason, or on which is right or wrong, but on something quite different called *iji o haru,* which could be translated as 'persisting in one's position' or 'showing the strength of ones sincerity" (Buruma, 10).

But many historians believe that the code of ethics prescribed for the samurai was influenced not only by *iji o haru,* but by the loyalty he exhibited toward his master through *giri.*

In fact, Tesshi summarizes the virtues of a samurai from the Hagakure text (samurai bible) which attests to the extent of that loyalty: (1) To serve the lord (master) without consideration of self; (2) to accept the lord's decisions even to the detriment of oneself; (3) to have concern only for the lord's house (Tesshi, 236). Tesshi has pointed out that this set of moral codes, which originated among the Samurai, have had a profound influence on the Japanese sense of loyalty to the group, and have also contributed directly to the diminished sense of self which now exists in Japanese society (Tesshi, 234).

The primary objective of Samurai training is to "build up character" through a curriculum of Jujitsu (a gentle martial art), fencing, archery, horsemanship, calligraphy, literature, history and ethics. These pursuits helped the samurai to find "the way of the samurai" (Bushido). Only *chi* (wisdom), *jin* (benevolence), and *yu* (courage) would lead the samurai down the "path" to a good character (Nitobe, 94-96). A samurai with good character therefore had been indoctrinated into a system of ethics which included loyalties and values of others (namely, the master) above himself. Thus the introduction of the word *ninjo,* and the new ethical concept in the Feudalistic period of *harakiri* or "ritualistic suicide," a fate which all samurai faced if they dared to show that they had doubts about this loyalty (Tesshi, 234).

Even in modern Japan the obligations of one's *giri* over one's *ninjo* still exist:

> To honor the society's ethical codes requires suppression of one's feelings; but succumbing to *ninjo* will cause social censure. Caught in this dilemma, there are three alternatives; one, to suppress one's private feelings and honor moral principles; two, to close one's eyes from moral obligations and follow the dictates of one's feelings; and three, to annihilate oneself through committing suicide, being able to neither ignore the society's moral obligations nor suppress one's personal desires (Befu, 169-170).

The third has been chosen many times by Japanese, especially by Japanese writers who claim that is has been their only alternative. Many Japanese novelists have committed suicide to make the point that Japan allows for no outward expression of *ninjo* (unless one wants to be ostracized from the group) and therefore no way to express one's individual morality (Shimahara, 121).

The *iemoto* (a pre-World War II term for house) is another system of obligation in Japanese society and is exhibited most profoundly through the hierarchy of the traditional Japanese arts. *Iemoto* refers to a vertical hierarchy of relations existent in houses of nonfamily members, often called a ritualized kinship. An example of a traditional art in Japan that is founded by a "master of tea," whose name becomes synonymous with *iemoto* - he is the master and the house. The master takes in pupils, who, in return for his teaching artistic techniques and eventual certification in *Cha no yu* (the art of tea), pay fees to the "house" (Nakane, 61). Also the pupils are required to give their loyalty to no other *iemoto* of tea (house or master), thereby paying their debt of obligation to the "master."

There are different houses of koto (a Japanese musical instrument) for example, but a pupil belonging to one *iemoto* will not switch schools or even listen to other schools' performances, because the *iemoto* and the subsequent master-pupil relationship demand complete loyalty. This is behavior that pupils exhibit despite the thinking of their *ninjo*:

> "Such a behavior pattern fits nicely into the structural principle of the organization. One realizes here the far-reaching structural implications of the golden rule of Japanese ethics - 'No man can serve two masters'" (Nakane, 61).

Nakane is quick to point out that the traditional Japanese system of lifetime employment is a modern example of this ethical principle and the servants' loyalty (unto death) to his lord, is a feudalistic example (Nakane, 62). However, in modern society the company refers to itself as *uchi*, a word that also means "house." But the various schools of traditional art still refer to themselves as *iemoto*, because they are more embedded in the historical ethical ideals of Bushido.

At the heart of the Bushido code is the basic master-student relationship, and the traditional arts still embrace this relationship through the *iemoto* system. Individuals may gain membership into a school of shakuhachi (a bamboo flute) without any requirements, but must adhere to the accepted code of behavior in the *iemoto* (Shimahara, 30). The *iemoto* commands respect from the student, and the student learns through observation and imitation of the master's technique. It is not acceptable to change the master's method, or to ask questions of the master. The goal of the method is a spiritual self-transformation of the student's *ki* (spirit, consciousness, will, and emotion), which can be detected by the master's *kan* (intuition); the master decides when the student's character and skills are proficient. Then, once the student finishes his training, he has a timeless indebtedness to the master in the form of continuing fees and loyalty (Shimahara, 32).

It is my contention that Talent Education has assumed this "structural principle of organization" - the *iemoto* system - along with its inherent ethical codes of behavior. Talent Education, although a modern school (founded in 1948), was organized with the structure of *iemoto* in mind. Suzuki is the *iemoto*, to which students pay their fees, and show their loyalty, and from which they receive training, in order to actually "buy" (*kau*) or "change" (*kawaru*) their character for themselves. Furthermore, this *iemoto* system being of purely Japanese origin, cannot be totally fathomed by Western minds not familiar with the cultural consciousness surrounding its continuance.

This web of values and obligations I have just described is the cultural consciousness which allows Japanese individuals to find meaning. The group consciousness continues to exist despite the demands that are made on individual identities, because the group offers the only identity which is acceptable in society. One's individual *ki*, and one's kinship and non-kinship *uchi* systems are ideal for maintaining the *wa* of society. The sacrificial relationships described in *amae* behavior, as well as the ethical code of *on* are useful in maintaining relationships of mutual dependence found in the *iemoto* hierarchy. Thus, mutual dependence and reciprocal obligation among individuals contribute as well to the continued success of the *wa*.

These values and obligations explain much about the external behavior of the Japanese cultural personality, but not much about the internal cognition which underlies that behavior - that is, the unconscious spirit. The unconscious in Japanese cultural cognition lies in the realm of language, its structure, function, and subsequent usage within society.

The Cultural Unconscious

The Japanese language can be seen as the unconscious part of the Japanese cultural consciousness because it is used by individuals in a ritualistic manner that becomes second nature. The relationship of language to culture has been described by Sapir as something which "defines experience for us by reason of its formal completeness of our unconscious projections and of its implicit expectations into the field of experience" (Sapir, 1). In other words, language allows the cultural consciousness to persist in a subtle way; these subtleties in Japanese appear in the verbal and nonverbal as well as the written language. According to the Japanese psychologist Takeo Doi, language is an important facet in understanding a culture's personality: "The typical psychology of a given nation can be learned only through familiarity with it's native language. The language compromises everything which is intrinsic to the soul of a nation and therefore provides the best projective test there is for each nation" (Doi, 1973a, 15).

The language of Japan perpetuates the Japanese ideal of the *wa* and the hierarchical loyalty of *on* through a language of formalism, which affects consciousness through the unconscious.The components of formalism are (1) Spoken formalism, which deemphasizes the self and lacks logic and precision, and (2) written formalism, which is influenced by the etymological meaning of the written *kanji* and the societal value which assumes highly perceptive skills of the senses, including a kind of intuition called *kan* and a sense of at one-ness with nature. These will be best understood through a basic knowledge of the structure of the Japanese language.

At present the Japanese language is most similar to Korean or Mongolian (Reischauer, 387); however, linguists are divided as to the origin of the spoken language. The Japanese language is similar to both the Altaic and the Polynesian language groups, despite the scholarly division between these groups. Ono has listed nine similarities between Japanese and the Altaic languages, (Turkish, Hungarian, Tungus, Manchu, archaic Korean, and Finnish) (Ono ,19). The most important are those which contribute to the vagueness of the language as spoken. In Altaic languages, and in Japanese as well, there is no difference between singular and plural, no distinction between gender, no articles of speech, no clear distinction between the stems of nouns and adjectives, and many verb forms are used as nouns (Ono, 19; Reischauer, 388). These similarities are interesting in light of what many observers have called the lack of logical or sequential structure in Japanese cognition and language.

Logical thought in the Japanese language has been influenced by Buddhism, in that it emphasizes aesthetics and a way of life which is artistic. Where science is concerned, concentration is upon particular facts, not universal principles. Therefore,

> Japanese expressions focus the thought and expression of the person on immediate concrete details of life. This tendency is quite unique to the Japanese. That is why the Japanese way of thinking habitually avoids summations of separate facts into broad statements about whole categories of things, although such abstraction is necessary for logical scientific thinking (Nakamura, 191-192).

Western logic as we know it is not used in any recognizable way among the Japanese, and this is because of the way in which they use the language. There could be two reasons for this difference: either (1) the Japanese language is not capable of expressing the logic of Western tongues because of the inherent grammatical structure or, (2) the language is valued for its intuitive and aesthetic expressions. Nakamura believes the latter to be true:

> "one actually can express oneself as clearly in Japanese as in any other language. . .However, the value of ways of Japanese expression lies more in aesthetic and intuitive aspects than in exactly logical ones" (Nakamura, 191).

Reischauer agrees with this point and states that the Japanese language has all the capabilities of being logical and concise in spite of the way it is used by the Japanese. He says that they actually prefer subtle and vague usages because they ensure harmony by avoiding opposites, thereby avoiding arguments and opposition among individuals (Reischauer, 387). To speak logically (in the Western sense) means to bring up in conversation the possibility of opposites, thereby raising questions which would only be detrimental to the harmony of the group. The stability of the *wa* is dependent upon this aspect of formalism which is a traditional pattern of communication. Nakamura quotes the Japanese scholar Motoori Noringa (1730-1801):

> In ancient times, we had no talk at all even about the way. The classic of Kakinomoto declares that in our land covered with reed and rice-ears, they have not argued since the time of the gods. To argue means not to expatiate or have much talk as is the custom in foreign countries (Nakamura, 189).

The avoidance of opposing forces and the avoidance of words in general were both highly valued in Noringa's era, and the values haven't changed much in contemporary society. For example, the Japanese language reflects the importance of the group and the relative unimportance of the individual through the exclusion of the pronoun "I" in speech. In some cases it is awkward and inappropriate to say "I" (Nakane, 35). Even to say, "I like that," is considered too brash in the Japanese language. If you like something, you merely say, "Suki desu" ("Like it"). In contrast to the English usage of the word "I" this whole idea seems rather bizarre, but even more bizarre is the fact that Japanese speakers may converse for hours without a spoken reference to a single subject. Furthermore, many times the subject of reference changes in mid sentence. Examples of this go back to Chinese Buddhist texts which the Japanese borrowed from China and rewrote in the Heian period. Nakamura suggests that the reason the Japanese can dispense with the first person is because the close bond they feel with other Japanese is used to intuit the reference in each case (Nakamura, 186). But this does not explain the reason for such use in literature, and in philosophy texts.

The Japanese word *kobutsu* (individual) was coined only after the introduction of Western logic to Japan, and serves as a reminder that the Japanese language has no precise words for the various states of being of an individual. In fact, Professor Inatomi has concluded after much research into the function of the Japanese language "that it is the perfect symbol of the Japanese people in its peculiarity of lacking a definite sense of the individual sense of self" (Tesshi, 235).

If the language is lacking in self-consciousness, it is certainly not lacking in group consciousness, especially in regard to the hierarchy of human relationships. Relationships within Japanese society demand the proper linguistic expression of individuals. Therefore, what is communicated and how it's communicated are dependent on to whom one is speaking. Undeniably spoken Japanese has traditionally contained a great wealth of expressions which denote relative social position. . .Every expression made by one person to another automatically sets the speaker in a relationship to the second as being superior, inferior, or equal (Yamagiwa, 205).

This system of ranking, or the seniority system, exists in every facet of society and requires the use of honorifics and appropriate verbal endings. Whether speech is formal or informal is determined by whether the person is higher or lower on the social ladder (Nakane, 31). In this way, what Westerners might refer to as "freedom of expression" is limited by the requirements of formalism. In Japan people attach far more importance to human feelings and the hierarchy of relationships than to reason or any universal moral system. There is no God, outside or above society watching us all. Instead, there is a complex system of etiquette, rules of behavior to fit specific social situations. . .Society itself is God, we are continually watched by other people. Hell as Sartre said, really is the others, although to many Japanese it seems more like Heaven" (Buruma, 11).

Individuals are thus limited by a group order which includes the delicacies of hierarchical language in society. It is sanctioned by the members, but also criticized for its strict regulation. The Japanese language is used to maintain the harmony and has had some interesting, if not evolutionary, effects on Japanese cognition.

The cognition, logic, and socialization behind what is said in Japanese are not even comparable to Western thought nor can these be properly translated into English. One must truly think like a Japanese in order to be fluent in the Japanese language because "Japanese cognition is characterized by concrete perception, a reliance on sensory data, and a high sensitivity to environmental context and relationships, whereas Western cognition involves logical sequential connections and the use of abstractions to represent universals" (Doktor, 32).

What Doktor has said of Japanese cognition is based on hemispheric studies comparing Japanese-speaking subjects to English-speaking subjects. The Japanese psychologist and linguist Tsunoda Tadonobu, has been comparing these groups since 1972. The basic premise of his research is that the Japanese language has influenced the thought processes of the Japanese brain in quantitative way. Not only are the hemispheric patterns for verbal language different from those of all other languages, excluding the Polynesian languages, but this difference is a direct result of the evolution of the Japanese and Polynesian languages. The implication is that the neurophysical components related to the auditory sense can be altered by language acquisition (Sibitani, 24).

The most important similarity between Japanese and Polynesian tongues is the five distinct vowel sounds which are present in both languages (Ono, 20). Reischauer has said that

> "Japanese, next to Polynesian, is phonetically one of the simplest languages in the world. It only has five standard Latin vowels a, i, u, e, and o, all pronounced as these are in Italian, Spanish or German" (Reischauer, 388).

The use of these five vowel sounds results in only twenty-three phonemes in Japanese, in contrast to English, which has forty-six. These facets of the Japanese phonetical structure began to be seen as important when Tsunoda began doing research on Japanese cognition in relation to the language that they speak. Vowels in the Japanese language can have meaning in themselves, a fact which Tsunoda demonstrated by making up this sentence of vowels, "Ue o ui, oi o ooi, ai o ou, aiueo," ("Worrying about hunger, disguising his old age, he chases love, a love-starved man") (Brabyn, 8).

Tsunoda describes the Japanese language as a vowel-dominant language, and says that because of the nature of the vowels, Japanese tend to become more

HEMISPHERIC COMPARISON OF AUDITORY FUNCTIONS

Japanese Lateralization

Left **Right**

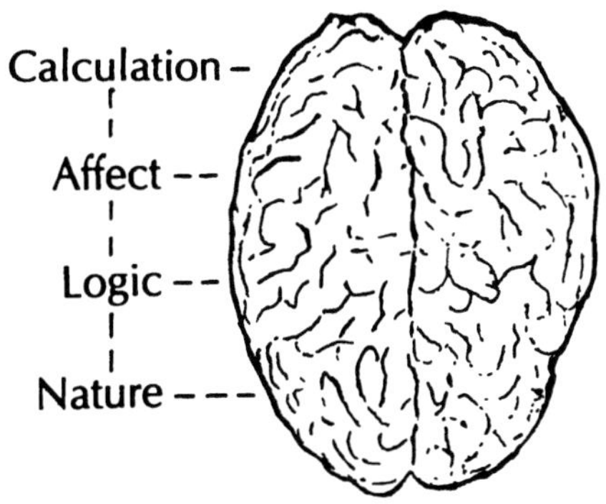

Left	Right
Speech-	
Vowels-	
Non-Verbal Human Sounds-	
Consonants-	
Human Voices-	
Animal Voices-	
	-Mechanical Sounds
Traditional Japanese-Instrumental Music	
	-Western Music

Western Lateralization

Left **Right**

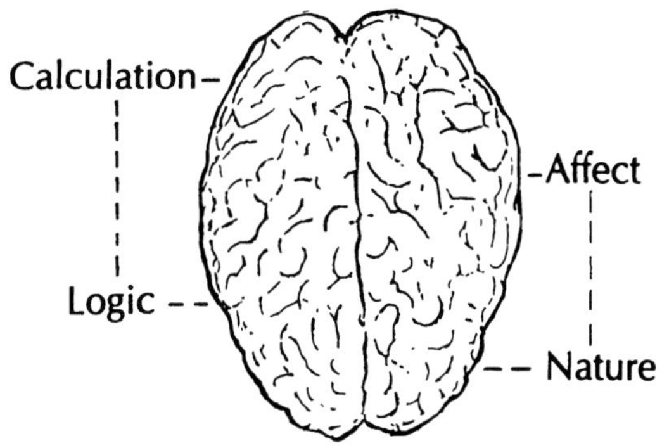

Left	Right
Speech –	
	-Vowels
	-Non-Verbal Human Sounds
Consonants –	
	-Human Voices
	-Animal Voices
	-Mechanical Sounds
	-All Instrumental Music

reliant upon auditory sense than do speakers of Western languages. Because this difference in initial language acquisition is due to what the Japanese encounter aurally, Tsunoda embarked on an experiment which culminated in a new theory and a book, Nihonjin no no (The Japanese Brain) (Sibitani, 25).

In this book Tsunoda describes the differences between the division of hemispheric function in native Japanese speakers and native speakers of seventeen other tongues (including English, Spanish, German, Chinese, [Canton, Taiwan, Peking, and Shanghai dialects], Vietnamese, Thai, Hebrew, Indonesian, French, Italian, Swedish, Polynesian, and African). Of these languages only the Polynesian natives (including Eastern Samoan, Maori, and Tonganese) exhibited the same left-brain dominance for sounds as did the Japanese speakers.

What Tsunoda was able to show was that the left cerebral hemisphere in the Japanese is dominant not only for verbal sounds but for most other sounds that the Japanese are subject to hearing, including Japanese pronounciated vowels (which are processed in the right hemisphere of non-Japanese subjects) and sounds of pure tone. The only sounds heard in the right hemisphere of native Japanese are man-made noises or mechanical sounds, and the sounds of Western music and instruments (Sibitani, 25).

Another interesting aspect of this auditory research is that the left hemisphere in Japanese subjects processes nonverbal human sounds which are emotive expressions - sounds like crying, sighing, or laughing. These emotional sounds are processed in the right hemisphere of non-Japanese subjects. The organized left half of the the Japanese brain also receives sounds of traditional Japanese instruments, as well as sounds of nature, animals, and insects (Brabyn, 6).

The Western brain also has a left hemisphere which is orderly and sequential, but in contrast it processes only the sounds of language and consonants. The right hemisphere is responsible for all the other sounds Tsunoda tested for (see Figure 1), including the vowel sounds and pure tone (Brabyn, 6; Sibitani, 26). The right hemisphere among Westerners and other non-Japanese speakers handle the non verbal human sounds of emotional quality, is adept at processing parallel information, and it is also holistic, whereas the Japanese right brain lacks these qualities (Tucker, 185).

The major auditory difference between Polynesian/Japanese subjects and Western subjects is that both Polynesian and Japanese make use of what Tsunoda calls the "stead state vowel," meaning that each vowel is always used with the same pronunciation (Sibitani, 24). Tsunoda is convinced that because these vowels are the only common trait of both languages and because these exact steady-state vowels don't occur in any other language, the role of spoken language can change cognition within a linguistic group (Sibitani, 25).

Tsunoda carried out his experiments on American-born Japanese who had never spoken any language except English and found that they exhibited the same pattern of lateralization as all the non-Japanese groups. He also studied the reverse, the effects of the Japanese language upon Koreans and Americans born and raised in Japan. They showed the standard Japanese pattern of left-hemispheric dominance (Brabyn, 6).

There is a paradox here. Despite the lack of "logic" exhibited by Japanese language and cognition, they show more left hemisphere dominance than does Western cognition (Doktor, 34). Tsunoda suggests that since emotional functions, language reception, and logic are all controlled by the left hemisphere, the Japanese person often allows emotional stimuli to confuse the thought process: "The same processes apply to non-Japanese people with respect to their right brain dominance for emotion-related sounds and functions. It can therefore be said that the laterality of emotion is acquired through the mother tongue" (Brabyn, 8).

The unique hemispheric lateralization in regard to the Japanese language seems to be implied in the role of the Japanese cultural consciousness; it does not appear to be genetically oriented, but rather, linguistically oriented. Insofar as language acquisition is an auditory phenomenon which begins at an early age and at a relatively unconscious state in young children, it is possible that emotion and logic are influenced by its acquisition.

The Japanese language has been called expressive, emotive, and nonlogical as spoken, but a "tragedy of history" as written (Corwin, 8). The Japanese adopted Chinese ideographs during the Nara-Heian periods (710-1159); the confusion surrounding their adoption still exists today (Hearn, 14). This confusion stems from the basic problem that Chinese characters or *kanji* as they are called in Japan, were originated for Chinese, a language which couldn't be further from spoken Japanese in linguistic structure (Reischauer, 389).

Some of the *kanji* were adopted complete with their Chinese meanings. For example, the word *tao* in Chinese means "the way or path"; its character in Japanese is a direct borrowing from China's character, which is used in Japanese to represent *to* or *do* (the way or path).

Thus *shin* (God or Gods) and *to* (the way or path) need two characters to form the word *shinto* (the way of the Gods) (Corwin, 6-7). (See Kanji List). The principle of *tao* in Chinese philosophy has influenced the Japanese arts; even those which don't have the suffix *to* or *do* make reference to "the way of flower-arranging" (Ikebana, see Traditional Japanese Arts Glossary) or "the way of Noh." Most of the characters which were borrowed from China, however, were ascribed to Japanese words, but they had to use at least two *kanji* per word, depending on the number of syllables in the word. So the Japanese have changed the Chinese system so much that written Chinese and Japanese today don't have much resemblance in meaning or looks. However, all Japanese students learn the Chinese and the Japanese names for every *kanji* they learn to write.

When a language is written in pictographs, one learns the etymology of one's own language from an early age, and there are certain cognitive effects. For example, when a Japanese hears a word, he is bound to intuit or visualize not only that *kanji* but the actual etymological meaning of that word from the moment it is spoken. It is an unconscious meaning because one does not think about it, one knows it from having been in school and learned it - but still one is influenced by a different kind of meaning. Durkeim speaks of the role of both the written and the spoken as being an integral part of one's unconscious:

> "Language is not merely the external covering of a thought; it is also its internal framework. It does not confine itself to expressing this thought after it has once been formed; it also aids in making it" (Landar, 230).

This meaning has value for the Japanese unconscious because it reinforces the cultural bond that already exists. The bond stems in part from the well-known fact that Japanese is relatively little-known by "outsiders," and this maintains the solidarity of the *uchi.* The cultural bond is allowed to persist through the indoctrination process, or *shitsuke* (socialization), into the isolated, harmonious relationship of society. Individuals who have been properly *shitsuke*'d have no consciousness of it. An example is the education in writing characters.

Because Japanese writing is so difficult, children must spend eleven years in school just learning to read and write the *kanji* (Sugishita). One cannot just write the characters any way he wants to, there is a "way" to writing the language, just as there is a "way" to do the tea ceremony.

For example a child learning to write must follow the prescribed way of completing each character. There is an order to each stroke, and everyone does it the same way. The character *naka* (middle or inside) looks like this 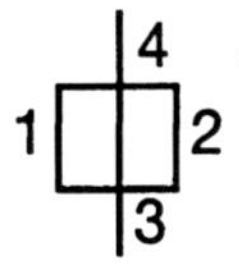

; the stroke order goes like this 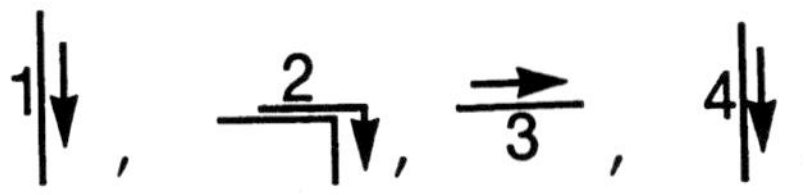

. After the *kanji* has been completed the average Westerner cannot tell what order the strokes were drawn in. However, in education this is an important aspect of learning to write: the stroke order is "the way" of writing. A very basic skill, but an important one - no one has reason to do it any other way. The value of writing the language is to be able to do it the same way, without thinking, every time you write; so that what began as a totally conscious effort becomes a totally unconscious effort (Taniuchi).

Through the spoken and written word, the Japanese live unconscious thoughts which add meaning to their existence, the facets of language keeping the cultural unconscious from becoming conscious. But the unconscious is valued to an even greater extent than that. Unconscious experience is something to be felt by individuals; such experience has value not for society but the for the individual. This is the realm of the Japanese "self." And the spirit of the unconscious allows individuals at last to find meaning. This is done without language, without thinking, and in a prescribed way.

The culmination of unconscious values in the Japanese language exists in the unseen, the unheard, and the unspoken which actually become meaningful through *mu* (nothingness). *Mu* is an aesthetic principle referring to space, air, or blankness, through which a person can feel or intuit meaning (D.T. Suzuki, 1967, 126). In the *mu* of a Shinto shrine, for example, there is no altar to look at, no priest to talk to, only a space in which to feel.

The *mu* is intuited through *kan,* roughly translated as "one's intuition," but actually it has a deeper meaning. *Kan* is doing without thinking, feeling without using the five senses, and learning through intuition. Furthermore, *kan* must be worked at, although, like rolling over in one's sleep, it is also a natural and unconscious characteristic (Taniuchi). Ultimately *kan* is the way to interpret the *mu,* in order for one's *ki* (spirit) to become enlightened.

In linguistic communication *mu* refers to those spaces between what is spoken, the actual feelings of the unsaid as intuited by the communicants (Nakamura, 180). What is not there often is meaningful for the Japanese. A good example of this is Japanese haiku:

Yado no haru	*A hut in spring:*
Nani mo naki koso	*There is nothing in it-*
Nani mo are	*There is everything*

(Behn, 33)

To become "enlightened" is to become empty, like the hut, only to be filled up again when you enter that state of *mu-shin* (no-mind) (D.T. Suzuki, 1959, 77). The state is compared again and again by D.T. Suzuki to the state of nature because nature lacks all consciousness and thought. "Man is a thinking reed, but nature is a mere reed." Man and nature have the reed in common; therefore, "nature is already Man, or otherwise no Man could come out of it. It is ourselves who fail to be conscious of the fact" (D.T. Suzuki, 1959, 248). The important part of man is the unconscious "reed"; this "reed" is the stationary axle, the unconscious state which man seeks through Zen experience, in order to become one with nature. It is for this reason that Zen is called a nonintellectual philosophy: to think is to take part in conscious reality and this interferes with one's ultimate goal of *mu-shin* (empty mind).

This state of "no-mind" in Zen philosophy transcends conscious reality in order to become unconscious. The experience has connotations of selflessness, which baffles the Westerner who is concerned with "being" - or bringing all into the realm of conscious experience. For this reason, the individual "Spirit of Japan" is difficult for the Westerner to capture. But through experience in Zen or the traditional arts, the spirit can be felt, and intuited. The Japanese believe that the artistic process brings about individual consciousness through *mu-shin*:

> "The aim of all the artistic discipline in Japan gathers around the self-appreciation of it, which is at once its own realization. "Mu-shin" or effortlessness is thus the consummation of art" (D.T. Suzuki, 1956, 290).

Dimensions in Talent Education Experience

Three dimensions of the Talent Education experience in Japan make it unique. The first is Suzuki himself. His cultural and personal history are the foundations upon which Talent Education rests. He is responsible for the origin and development of the Talent Education *iemoto*. The second is the mother-child relationship in Japanese society, and the historical attitudes about the education of both. The third dimension is the master-student relationship in Talent Education system. This includes my personal experiences and interpretations of his philosophy.

The Origin and Development of the Talent Education *Iemoto*

The workings of Talent Education in Japan are invariably linked to certain aspects of the Japanese cultural consciousness because Suzuki has devised a system of education that encompasses Eastern values, obligations, and philosophy. Talent Education is a method which no one pays much attention to in Japan (Suzuki is relatively unknown in his country) because it creates no controversy. The violin was originally the only instrument used in Talent Education, but now the method encompasses a variety of Western stringed instruments. "Western" is the key word here - if Suzuki had devised the same system of education using a Japanese instrument, Talent Education would be just another *iemoto* (house system) of traditional art. Consequently he would still be unknown in the Western world as well.

Suzuki introduced the European violin into Japanese culture in the way which was most natural for him - through a system of education which he knew had worked in the traditional arts. But the origin and development of Talent Education by Suzuki did not occur in a vacuum; he was influenced by his interests in music, art, philosophy, and children before he created his *iemoto*. And his unique personality is inextricably a major part of the *iemoto* because not only is he the head of the *iemoto*, he is the *iemoto*. A study of his life experience in relation to his culture therefore becomes critical to the understanding of Talent Education's origin and development.

Erik Erikson in his book Life History and the Historical Moment, discusses the importance of understanding the personal history of an individual who has had an impact on his society and/or the world:

> Psychosocial identity, then, also has a psychohistorical side, and suggests the study of how life histories are inextricably interwoven with history. The study of psychosocial identity, therefore, depends on three complementaries - or are they three aspects of one complementarity? - namely, the personal coherence of the individual and role integration of his group; his guiding images and the ideologies of his time; his life history - and the historical moment (Erikson, 1955, 20).

Shinichi Suzuki's father, Masakichi Suzuki, was a samisen maker (see Traditional Arts Index) and a lower-class samurai at the time of Suzuki's birth, but just two years later Masakichi Suzuki opened the first violin factory in Japan. The violin had been introduced into Japan centuries before, but no one had tried to reproduce violins until this moment.

The early nineteen hundreds in Japan was a time of rapid influx of Western thought and ideas; the slogans of the Meiji era advocated that Western science be learned, but not at expense of the "Japanese Spirit," as this slogan by the Emperor Meiji states:

> **May our country,**
> **Taking what is good**
> **And rejecting what is bad,**
> **Be not inferior to any other.**

At the beginning of the Meiji era (1870s), Japanese began to shun their own culture, feeling ashamed of their lack of knowledge. They tried to make up for all those years of isolation by taking in all that was Western (Cleaver, 210). Masakichi was a young man at this time, not really a Samurai because Japan's feudalism was dying, he was a samisen maker like his father, but the societal emphasis was on the Western. Masakichi was influenced by this cultural emphasis, and his production of violins at the turn of the century can be seen as a direct outgrowth of the pervasive thought during that era (Kojima). During the 1890s this anti nationalism turned to nationalism again, and this is the cultural mindset which Suzuki grew up with.

Suzuki began playing the violin when he was sixteen. When he was eighteen he was chosen to be the companion of Prince Tokugawa. Companions were traditionally chosen from the lower class, but were supposed to exhibit "high breeding" (Kojima). This experience changed the course of Suzuki's life. He traveled with the Prince and the Tokugawa family and lived in Tokyo mansions until he went to Germany.

While in Tokyo he studied the violin, but he wanted to study the violin in a country with a long tradition of violin training. He says in his book Nurtured by Love that he wanted to learn what art really was, not necessarily to become a "great musician." Suzuki had been expected to stay in Japan to take over his father's business, which was now at the height of its prosperity. In fact, his father had asked that Suzuki not go to Germany, and Suzuki had begrudgingly agreed. But it was the Prince who devised a plan to get Suzuki to Germany. The Prince had been planning a world cruise, and Suzuki was supposed to go with him. Suzuki would be left off close to Germany and the Prince would deal with Suzuki's father (Kojima; Suzuki, 1969).

In 1920, Suzuki found himself in Berlin, where he studied violin with Klinger for ten years. The Meiji thinking which permeated Japan from 1900 to 1920 was as much responsible for Suzuki's trip to Germany as was the Prince. Suzuki wanted to take in something good from another culture, he wanted to learn about art: "My ultimate desire was not to become a performer but to understand art" (Suzuki, 1969, 76).

When Suzuki returned to Japan in 1930, he found a very changed country. Western ideals had permeated public education in science, organization, and technology. Japan, he felt, was losing much of her traditional character as a result of diminishing emphasis in education on character formation. This was the beginning of Suzuki's concern for educational ideals. In his absence numerous traditional Japanese values had undergone changes (Kojima).

Erik Erikson has said that "historical crises, in turn, aggravate personal crises" (Erikson, 1975, 22). The changes which had taken place in Japan had a profound effect upon Suzuki. He was concerned that the traditional values of Japan had been replaced with the new technology of the West. In fact, it later became Suzuki's contention that it was this type of education, the overconcern for knowledge and the underconcern for character, which brought Japan into the crisis of war.

After his return to Japan, Suzuki and his three brothers formed the Suzuki Quartet, which became well known throughout Japan. He also became a disciple of Sensei (teacher) Mizumura, from whom he learned Ichigen dōka (The first path). The focus of his training was his *ki*. Through meditation and concentration, he began his search for *ki* (spirit or character) and *kan* (unconscious or intuition), which were thought to be the only way to the pure Zen mind or *mu-shin*.

One year later he and another music teacher founded Teikoku Ongaku (the Imperial Conservatory) in Tokyo. Suzuki was teaching college-age students until a man came to his studio with his four-year-old son and asked Suzuki to please teach him the violin (Suzuki, 1969). Suzuki said he needed time to think about the proposition, since he had never considered teaching children before. Soon after this visit, Suzuki remarks, "it hit me like a flash: all Japanese children speak Japanese. . .Why not apply this method to other faculties?" (Suzuki, 1969).

This new idea, combined with his love for the violin and his concern for the training of character, can be seen as a new personal crisis for Suzuki. For the next eleven years he experimented with children ranging from 3 to 7 years old; he had already begun to make education his life's work before the war began. During those years he said he began to see all of the goodness in children of this age. "They know how to love, trust, live joyfully, they have no fear, and they love justice" (Suzuki, 1969, 65). These qualities of children he refers to as their "natural life force," in other words their *ki* or character, and he often talked about his desire to become like them.

He still talks about the *ki* of children today. *Ki* is the life force within all humans which can be felt by others who possess it through their *kan* or intuition. Suzuki has said,

> I am often misunderstood and some adults make faces, but it is possible that children come to me because I radiate respect for them. . . Love and Respect combined is what establishes a bond. . .Everyone loves children. I respect children as my teachers (Suzuki, 1981, 38).

This respect for children and the ultimate concern for their *ki* or character led Suzuki to write many books on the subject of education (See List of Suzuki's Writings). His first book, entitled Strong Education, was published in 1941 and was censored by the highly nationalistic government of Japan. This may explain the title of the book. His second book, *Talent Education for Young Children [Yoji no Saino Kyoiku to Sono Hoho]*, was written partially before and partially after the war. In this book Suzuki says that the success of Japan depends upon the education of its people. This book can be seen as the culmination of his thoughts and experiences, and remains the basis for his thinking today. I am indebted to Masami Kojima for the initial translation of the following points from Talent Education for Young Children.

Suzuki called for a change in the educational system in Japan. The new system would be built on the following beliefs:

1. Children would begin their educational training at three or four years of age. Education which begins at age seven misses the most critical age for character development. He cited the hundred children aged three to five to whom he had taught the violin as evidence that education by the mother-tongue method works. He asserted that listening, imitating, and memorizing were the only skills needed to further education in any area.

2. The causes of the war stemmed from bad education during the Meiji and Taisho eras. The education of those eras lost sight of training the *ki* (character) of children.

3. Japanese people have begun to believe that talent is inborn, and they don't understand how ability can be cultivated through education.

4. Talent Education was the type of education which would ultimately save the nation and the world.

5. Women held the future of Japan in their hands, depending on how they used their new right to vote in the country. Women should realize now as they used to that the education of children is of paramount importance to them and to the existence of the nation.

6. Suzuki suggested that the country found a special kindergarten, in which a system of Talent Education would be practiced. Children three to seven years old would be required to go. (Ultimately it was the American/Allied occupation that decided upon the new system of education for Japan.)

7. Each child would choose a subject from the curriculum and study it exclusively until elementary school, where he would begin to study other areas. His idea was that a child who has mastered "the way of math" or "the way of sculpture" would be able to learn other disciplines easier once discipline and ability had been achieved in one area.

8. He continually talked of different disciplines as the Zen masters talked about the traditional arts education in "the way of the sword" or "the way of nature." He had been profoundly influenced by his study of *ki* and *kan* and thought that these concepts held the key to all educational practices, and the fate of humanity. Education, he believed was character training, not merely "teaching."

The decline in education which Suzuki noticed upon his return from Germany can be understood through Dore's distinction between "education" and "qualification":

> Education involves changing people: it depends on awakening, and sustaining by a continuous process of partial satisfaction and further stimulation, curiosity and the desire for self-development, the desire to understand, the desire to achieve, and the desire to master. . . Qualification on the other hand is merely instrumental, the passive absorption of ready-made answers in order to become qualified, certified, and entitled to a job, a salary, and social status (Dore, 1965, 20).

The system of education which had been based on character education in the arts had changed significantly after the Second World War to the mere technical use of education to attain status and power. Although Suzuki's book was not a success in Japan, five businessmen in Matsumoto who had heard of his quartet and his work with children asked him to come and conduct the Matsumoto orchestra. Eventually, Suzuki convinced the men to help him open a school of music for young children. In 1948, the Talent Education Institute (the *iemoto*) was set up in Matsumoto, and Suzuki became the apex of the *iemoto* hierarchy, the "violin master."

Suzuki's attitudes toward education have changed only slightly since 1946. About his forty years of teaching with of the mother-tongue method, he says, "I learned clearly that there is no inborn talent for music ability" (Suzuki, 1978, 4). Suzuki still wants to make changes in the education system in Japan and calls for a national policy of the mother-tongue method. Also, through the new International Suzuki Association, Suzuki hopes to create awareness in all countries. He says "it is one of the most urgent problems of our time, and appears to be mankind's major blindspot" (Suzuki, 1973, 18).

The reason for this blind spot, he says is that no one understands the function of art:

> There are people who insist that art exists for its own sake, but I do not think so. Art exists for the human species. I think that all of the people who love art, those who teach art, and all of you should burn with the obligation to save the world. To achieve this it is necessary to be concerned about the importance of educating a really beautiful human spirit (Suzuki, 1981, 61).

Talent Education of the Mother and Child

There are historical beliefs about and attitudes toward early education that are reflected in the success of Talent Education in Japan. Traditional training of children in Medieval Japan began on *okeiko goto* (June sixth of a child's sixth year). This is in fact equivalent to four or five years of age, because before World War II the system for counting a child's age was different. A child was one year of age on his day of birth and two years old on the next New Year.

In Kodensho, a book on *noh* drama dating back to 1200 A.D. (the Kamakura period in Japan), it is said that the training of actors should begin no later than seven years of age (actually five or six). By comparison, Philippe Aries in his book Centuries of Childhood observes that in medieval Europe there was an emphasis on education before the age of twenty, but never a belief that a younger age was a better age.

In Japan, the idea is still prevalent that a child's education should begin with early lessons and preschool at the age of four or five. In fact, Japan has the highest preschool enrollment of any other country in the world excluding France. Most of the preschools are parent supported. Many parents believe that languages, music, and physical movement can best be taught at early ages, because they foster fine motor skills and coordination (Hayashi).

Before the war only the noble classes of samurai educated their young in the traditional arts, but most people believed in the benefits of early education (Taniuchi). Public sentiment traditionally idealized early character training in the traditional arts.

The education of the young included the immediate participation of the mother. In the 1800s, a book entitled Onna Daigaku [Great Learning for Women], stated that a woman must be responsible enough to purify her children, because the mother and child are linked by the heart. Suzuki has said the same thing in Nurtured by Love, that a woman must *hansei* (purify or introspect) her own heart, in order to purify the child's heart (Suzuki, 1981). These ideals for women and mothers are embedded in a folk belief called *taikyo,* which in essence says that women's moods and feelings from the moment of conception are going to be the child's moods and feelings because the two are linked by the heart (Dore, 1965, 133).

When the Meiji reforms of 1822 allowed for the education of women in Japan, the goals remained traditional. Women's education was to consist of character training in "the arts" and in "the workings of the human heart" (Cleaver, 212).

In modern Japan the role of the mother in the child's education has not changed much in theory, but the increased demands made on her at present are a direct outgrowth of the Meiji ideal that the mother is responsible for he child's nurturance. When Suzuki says that "man is the son of his environment," he is saying that children are dependent upon their mothers for their ultimate development as good human beings.

This puts a lot of pressure on the Japanese mother in Talent Education to work with her child. The mother probably works harder that the child because the child's progress is thought to reflect directly on her.

In Japanese public education as well as Talent Education, the transition from home to school is made easier by the mother. First the child goes to the potential school and observes the older students in their classes. The practice is called *minarai* (watch and learn), and it is done about one month prior to the actual going to classes or lessons. Suzuki suggests that if the child wants to learn he will learn easily because he is hungry for learning. Therefore the mother must motivate the child through a process called *Iyoku zukuri* (appetite making) (Taniuchi).

This process of "appetite making" is used extensively throughout the rest of the child's education. For example, a junior high school student interested in joining the tennis club is first asked to *minarai* the other students at play, or perhaps sweep the tennis courts before practice. He is to wait patiently until the group is ready to accept him. Then when the chance has finally arrived for him to become a member of the team, or the school, or the *iemoto,* he is both excited and grateful. Becoming a part of the group gives him an identity and a purpose.

When he is accepted into the group, his equipment comes from the club, school, or *iemoto* (Taniuchi). This ideal operates in most organized hierarchical systems in Japan, including Talent Education. The child is given a violin not by his parents, but by the *sensei* (teacher). In the traditional forms of musical arts, too, the pupil was always presented with his instrument as a gift from the master. Furthermore, the student was not allowed to own his own instrument until he was a mater of his art (Suzuki, 1959, 211).

The master is the supreme artist, he is an "artist of life," something the pupils want to become. Therefore the student will endure anything and study, without question, whatever the master tells him to study (Dore, 1965, 15).

Sensei-Gakusei (Master-Student) and *Do* (the Way)

The spirit of the traditional arts is the Zen philosophy, whose ideal is to show individuals "the way" to *mu-shin*. Arts education has nothing to do with what Westerners would call "creativity," but through the arts the Japanese individual can find self-expression. However, there is a path of discipline in the form of a method, which must be followed at the expense of the individual's *ninjo* (personal feelings). For example, there is the belief in Japanese arts education that a student should simply, without question, do as the master asks. Through the act of doing, he will get a feel for the act, and once he feels it, he'll understand why he had to do it without question. The simultaneous acts of doing and feeling allow the individual to become egoless, artless, and pure in heart (Taniuchi). The method is prescribed by the master, and the student is there not to attain mastery of the art itself, but to become a Zen "artist of life" (Dore, 15). The transformation of the ego is seen as essential to this attainment.

According to D. T. Suzuki, "To study Zen means to have Zen experience" (Suzuki, 1967, 124). A Zen experience brings about a personal transformation which must be related to others; this is the goal of Zen experience in the traditional arts. In the beginning I quoted Suzuki as saying "Study means change, I change myself - this is study." Similar to Suzuki's concept is Zen experience in Buddhism, which states that "everything in the world arises, changes, and perishes; nothing remains constant for even a single moment" (Corwin, 44). If we see the world as undergoing continuous change, then we come closer to the ideal of the Zen mind. *Mu-shin* is the ultimate goal for individuals in the arts. When this state of unconsciousness is realized, "there is no sense of 'I am doing it'. The feeling of 'self' is a great hindrance to the execution of a work" (D.T. Suzuki, 1956, 290). Suzuki says this also: "The conscious attempt to play well detracts from the working of *kan* (Suzuki, 1981, 43). During lessons with teachers, Suzuki often goes through this dialogue:

Suzuki: Please, you must say, "I don't play".

Student: I don't play.

Suzuki: I hope so. [meaning, I hope you're right]

If the piece sounded forced, Suzuki would interrupt with:

Suzuki: Bow plays better. Take off yourself, bow plays violin.

And if there was still no progress he would pick up his violin, put it on his shoulder and say,

Suzuki: Bow plays better than I, without bow I can't play.

One plays through his *kan* by "taking off" himself. In Zen, the "I" is consciousness - the "thinking reed" - but conscious thought interferes with man's true Buddha-nature, which is the unconscious reed. The violin and the bow are a part of nature, the unconscious reed. The violin is made of maple or spruce, the strings of metal or animal gut, and the bow of wood and animal hair. The violin is already at one with itself; it is the violinist who must transcend his thinking by taking off the "I," and becoming a mere reed. The violin and bow need the violinist because the bow cannot play the violin by itself. Similarly the violinist could not play the violin without nature; nature is the bow, the violin, and the violinist. Suzuki often asked, "How would violin sound if bow could play violin? Please play this way."

The bow can play the violin much better without the help of "I," and one gets rid of "I" through the unconscious state of *mu-shin*. There is no "I" in *mu-shin* just as there is no "I" in the group. There is no "I" in the traditional arts, yet the arts are intended to help individuals find self-expression. Ultimately in Japanese society there is no "I" used in the self-expression of individuals because individuals use their *kan* (unconscious intuition) to intuit meaning among themselves.

Sometimes Suzuki would have a student hold out his bow arm, with the bow in it, and then he would draw an imaginary line from the tip of the bow to the student's heart. "Your arm is bow, and bow goes to heart. When you understand this - then you will become tone." I always laughed at his bad English. But as time passed and he repeated this phrase again and again, I realized that he did expect the tone to live through me. The tone and I were to "become" one. A *shuji* painting that he gave me sums up the ideal, "Tone with living soul."

In <u>Zen and the Art of Archery</u>, Herrigel notes the importance of the master in guiding the student to forget himself and transform himself:

> nobody can stay the course without conscientious guidance from a skilled teacher and without the help of a Master. No less decisive, on the other hand, is the fact that his experiences, his conquests and spiritual transformations, so long as they still remain 'his', must be conquered and transformed again and again until everything is annihilated (Herrigel, 22).

I couldn't quite understand how a person could be in an unconscious state and still play the violin. Suzuki wanted me to play the violin, and not play the violin. Spiritually, he wanted me to remove myself from what I had spent twenty-one years "getting into," and physically he wanted me to forget my body and become part of the violin and bow. I didn't want to listen to Suzuki because his concepts were backward from anything I'd ever experienced. I decided I could do without him.

But as Herrigel said, "No one can stay the course without a master," and I was about to learn from firsthand experience that the master-student relationship demands a dependency on the part of the student. The dependency relationship between the master and student is an extension of the most fundamental relationship in Japanese society - the *amae* relationship of the mother and the child. The student's role is the one of the child, and the master's role is that of the mother (Doi, 1973a, 10). The master, like the mother, has trained for his role, and can intuit the heart of the student. The master understands what the student is ready for and when, as Herrigel relates in his experience with the art of archery:

> "The Master knows you and each of his pupils much better than we know ourselves. He reads in the soul of his pupils more than they care to admit" (Herrigel, 21).

For the first three months, I couldn't play the simplest music because I was concentrating on the different aspects of posture, tone production, and breathing. Herrigel states that his frustration in learning the art of archery was worse the first year because of the pains in learning the correct posture and breathing techniques.

> "You cannot do it because you do not breathe right. . .through this breathing you will not only discover the source of all spiritual strength but will also cause this source to flow more abundantly, and to pour more easily through your limbs" (Herrigel, 29).

Suzuki asked me to "try breathing as if the violin itself needs a breath." He gave me breathing exercises which interfered with my posture and my playing. I finally got to the point where I couldn't touch the violin because I was afraid I would do something wrong. Then I convinced myself that I couldn't play the violin, let alone ever teach the violin to children. "I" gave up. The "I" was removed from the violin, and now Suzuki would work with me. In the act of giving up, "I" had admitted that I couldn't do it all myself. He had broken the barrier between us, and now I had to depend upon him. This was my only option now because we both knew I had nothing to lose; but as I was to find out, this was only the beginning. From this point forward, everything Suzuki said - especially in regard to tone production - was a metaphor for changing oneself.

In the training of shakuhachi (the Japanese bamboo flute), tone production is what studying the flute is all about. This is true of Talent Education as well. When Suzuki says, "Nice tone, nice heart" he means in order to have a good tone, you must change internally. One of the instructors at Talent Education warned students, "If you only imitate Dr. Suzuki's bowing superficially, you won't have the same tone." Tone is thought of as an internal expression which is not dependent on external technique, but the success of that technique is dependent upon the internal progression of one's heart. Suzuki had been using the ideal of tone as metaphor for a higher ideal.

In archery, "the bow and arrow are only a pretext for something that could just as well happen without them" (Herrigel 18). In Talent Education the violin and bow are only *do* ("the way") to the goal, but the goal itself is internal change, continual transformation of the self. This is character (*ki*) training. Suzuki shows his students how to change themselves so they can "bring up" children who will change the world.

TRADITIONAL JAPANESE ARTS GLOSSARY

Aikido - a Japanese martial art (literally "the way of harmonizing body and spirit")

Cha no yu - a stylized way of preparing tea which orginated in fifteenth century

Haiku - a seventeen-syllable poem, divided into three lines of five, seven, and five, respectively

Ikebana - the art of flower arranging which orginated in Shinto and Buddhist philosophy, but became an art in the fourteenth century

Judo - a Japanese martial art (literally "the way of softness")

Kabuki - a stylized drama which was developed by the seventeenth century merchant class

Karate - a Japanese martial art (literally "empty-handed")

Koto - a thirteen-stringed instrument traditionally played by Japanese women

Nihonto - the Japanese sword

Noh - a drama where all the actors are men, and music, dancing, and masks are used to depict stories of mythological or historical significance

Samisen - a three-stringed banjo-like instrument with no frets

Shakuhachi - a five-holed vertical flute made of bamboo which orginated in China

Shuji - stylized writing or calligraphy

Sumie - ink painting

Ukiyoe - woodblock printing or "pictures of the fleeting world" as they were called by the seventeenth century merchants who originated the art

KANJI (character) LIST

WORD (in Romaji)		***KANJI*** (and literal translations)		***ENGLISH TRANSLATION***
SAINO	***Sai***	才	***Genius, Talent***	*TALENT ABILITY*
	No	能	***Ability, Noh Drama***	
GAIJIN	***Gai,***	外	***Outside***	*FOREIGNER*
	Jin	人	***Person***	
SHINTO	***Shin,***	神	***God***	*THE WAY OF THE GODS*
	Kami To	道	***Way or Path***	
BOIN	***Bo***	母	***Mother***	*VOWEL*
	In	音	***Sound***	
SENSEI	***Sen***	先	***Future***	*TEACHER/MASTER*
	Sei	生	***Life***	
GAKUSEI	***Gaku***	学	***Learn***	*STUDENT*
	Sei	生	***Life***	
MONSEI	***Mon***	門	***Gate***	*PUPIL/DISCIPLE*
	Sei	生	***Life***	
UCHI	***Uchi***	内	***Inside, House***	*INSIDE*
AMAE	***Ama(i)***	甘	***Sweet, Indulgence***	*MUTUAL DEPENDENCE*
	Ama(eru)		***Presume upon another's love***	
NINJO	***Nin***	人	***Person, Human***	*EMPATHY*
	Jo	情	***Emotion, Sympathy***	
GIRI	***Gi***	義	***Duty***	*MORAL OBLIGATION*
		理	***Reason, Logic***	
ONGAKU	***On***	音	***Sound***	*MUSIC*
	Gaku	楽	***Music/Pleasure, Enjoyment***	
NIHON	***Ni***	日	***Sun***	*JAPAN*
	Hon	本	***Origin***	
KOKORO		心	***Heart, Mind Soul***	*HEART*
IEMOTO		家	***House***	*MASTER*
		元	***Origin***	
KI	***Ki***	気	***Vapor***	*SPIRIT, SOUL MOOD*
KAN	***Kan***	勘	***Perception, Sixth Sense***	*INTUITION*
WA	***Wa***	和	***Peace, Harmony***	*HARMONY*

The Pre-historic Periods of Japan

The Preceramic Age	Late Pleistocene
The Jomon period	10,000 B.C.
The Yayoi period	300 B.C.
The Tomb period	250 B.C.

The Historical Periods of Japan

Nara period	710-794
Heian period	794-1185
Kamakura period	1185-1336
Muromachi period	1336-1568
Momoyama period	1568-1603
Edo period	1603-1868

Modern period

Meiji era	1868-1912
Taisho era	1912-1926
Showa era	1926-

CHRONOLOGY OF SUZUKI SHINICHI AND THE TALENT EDUCATION METHOD

1898 Suzuki born in Nagoya, Japan. His father, Masakichi Suzuki was a lower-class samurai, and samisen maker in the pre-Meiji era. His mother was a singer and samisen player.

1900 His father opened The Suzuki Violin Factory in Nagoya. The factory employed 1,100 workers and could produce 400 machine-made violins and 4,000 bows per day.

1918 Suzuki met Prince Tokugawa Marquis, and was chosen to be the Prince's companion.

1919 Suzuki stayed at the Tokugawa Mansion in Tokyo while taking violin lessons from Ando Ko.

1920 Prince Tokugawa took Suzuki to Germany by ship and Suzuki stayed in Berlin to study violin with Professor Klinger. During his ten year stay he became friends with Albert Einstein.

1928 Suzuki returned to Japan and formed the Suzuki Quartet with three of his brothers.

1929 Professor Kunnitachi and Suzuki formed Taikoku Ongaku Gakko (Imperial Music Conservatory) in Tokyo of which Suzuki was president.
He married a German woman, a singer from Berlin.
He became a disciple of Mizumura Sensei, who was a master of "Ichi gendo ka" (the way of *ki* and *kan*).

1932 Suzuki began teaching young children to play the violin using the Talent Education method. He taught nearly one-hundred students between 1932 and 1943.

1943 Suzuki moved to Kiso, Japan to work at his father's new violin factory which produced Geta (Japanese wooden thongs) during the war.

1944 Suzuki became ill and was bed-ridden in Asama, Japan, for two years. He was cured by Chinese medicine.

1946 Five Matsumoto businessmen asked Suzuki to become the conductor of the Matsumoto Amateur Orchestra and to be a judge for a local music competition. He began teaching at the Matsumoto music school instead, teaching young children.

1947 The Suzuki Violin Factory in Kiso began producing violins again.

1948 Talent Education School opened in Matsumoto, with a lot of money spent by the five Matsumoto businessmen. Suzuki began lecturing all over Honshu (the main Japanese island), and the periodical of Saino Kyoiku (Talent Education) was published.

1949 Branches of Talent Education were founded in Nagano, Nagoya, and Tokyo. Also, Suzuki ran for the School Board in Matsumoto, but lost.

1958 New Talent Education building was built in Matsumoto (it is the current structure). Professor Clifford Cook of Oberlin Conservatory viewed a film about Talent Education.

1964 Suzuki and a group of Japanese children toured the United States, and sparked the acceptance of what Americans call the Suzuki Method. Professor Cook began a Suzuki program at Oberlin and Professor John Kendall began a Suzuki program at the University of Southern Illinois. Professor Kendall was the first American to visit Talent Education in Matsumoto.

1965 Suzuki began training teachers in Talent Education, created Talent Education kindergartens in Matsumoto and Tokyo, and the various music methods in piano, cello, flute, viola and harp were added to the Violin Method. Tour children go to foreign countries every year with Suzuki to play concerts and spread the philosophy of Talent Education.

Writings of Shinichi Suzuki

1932 - Article for a book: "The Study of the Violin and the Bow."

1932 - Article for a book: "The History of Japanese Violin."

1936 - Article for a book: "Study of Keyser."

1937 - Magazine article: "Notes on the Bow."

1937 - Book: How Anyone Can Get a Correct Tone on the Violin

1941 - Book: Strong Education

1946 - Book: Talent Education for Young Children

1948 - Book: Talent Education

1951 - Book: How I Play

1954 - Book: The Fate of Children

1958 - Book: Method of Musical Expression

1960 - Book: The Philosphy and Techniques of Playing the Violin

1960 - Book: The Path I've Trod

***1966** - Book: Nurtured by Love: A New Approach to Education

***1969** - Book: Ability Development From Age Zero

***1982** - Book: Where Love Is Deep

**Note: Suzuki also has written for the Talent Education Journal from 1948 to the present. Available in English.

* Books translated into English

REFERENCES

Behn, Harry. Cricket Songs: Japanese Haiku. New York: Harcourt, Brace and World, 1964.

Benedict, Ruth. The Chrysanthimum and the Sword. Boston: Houghton Mifflin, 1946.

Brabyn, Howard. "Mother Tongue and the Brain." The Unesco Courier, February 1982: 5-8.

Buruma, Ian. A Japanese Mirror: Heros and Villains of Japanese Culture. London, Jonathan Cape: 1984.

Chew, John J. "The Japanese Language in the Eyes of Postwar Japan: A review article." Journal of Asian Studies, 18 (1984): 475-480.

"Children Have Forgotten How to Play." The Japan Times, 7 February 1984: P. 2.

Cleaver, Charles G. Japanese and Americans: Cultural Parallels and Paradoxes. Tokyo: Charles E. Tuttle, 1976.

Corwin, Charles. Biblical Encounter with Japanese Culture. Tokyo: Christian Literature Crusade, 1967.

Cummings, William K. Education and Equality in Japan. Princeton, N.J.: Princeton University Press, 1980.

Damasio, Antonio R. "Reflection on the Work of R.W. Sperry." Trends in Neurosciences, 5 (1982): 222-224.

Dobrin, Arnold. Igor Stravinsky: His Life and Times. New York: Thomas Y. Crowell, 1970.

Doi, Takeo. The Anatomy of Dependence. Tokyo: Kodansha International, 1973a.

Doi, Takeo. "The Japanese Patterns of Communications and the Concept of Amae." The Quarterly Journal of Speech, 56 (1973b): 180-185.

Doktor, Robert. "A Cognitive Approach to Culturally Appropriate HRD Programs." Training and Development Journal, October 1982: 32-36.

Dore, R.P. Education in Tokugawa Japan. Berkeley: University of California Press, 1965.

Dore, R.P. "The Legacy of Tokugawa Education," Edited by Marius B. Jansen. Changing Japenese Attitudes Toward Modernization. Princeton, N.J.: Princeton University Press, 1961.

Erikson, Erik H. Childhood and Society. Great Britain: Penguin Books, 1950.

Erikson, Erik H. Life History and the Historical Moment: Diverse Presentations. New York: W.W. Norton, 1975.

Friedrich, Otto. "What Do Babies Know." Time, 15 August 1983: 52-59.

Gabowitz, Louis. "Examining the Suzuki Approach." The Strad, June 1974: 73-79.

Galin, David, et al. "Development of the Capacity for Tactile Information Transfer Between Hemispheres in Normal Children." Science, 2046 (1979): 1330-1332.

Gardner, Howard. *Art, Mind and Brain.* New York: Basic Books, 1982.

Gardner, Howard. "Do Babies Sing a Universal Song?" Psychology Today, December 1981: 70-76.

Gardner, Howard. Frames of Mind: The Theory of Multiple Intelligences. New York: Basic Books, 1983.

Gardner, Howard. The Arts and Human Development: A Psychological Study of the Artistic Process. New York: John Wiley, 1973.

Gardner, Howard. "The Music of the Hemispheres." Psychology Today, June 1982: 392-392.

Garfinkel, Percy. "The Best 'Jewish Mother' in the World." Psychology Today, September 1983: 56-60.

Gordon, Ira J. Human Development: A Transactional Perspective. New York: Harper and Row, 1975.

Hanayama, Shinsho. "Buddhism of the One Great Vehicle (Mahayana)." The Japanese Mind: Essentials of Japanese Philosophy and Culture. Edited by Charles A. Moore. Tokyo: Charles E. Tuttle, 1967.

Hawkins, Robert D., and Eric O. Kandel. "Is There a Cell Biological Alphabet for Simple Forms of Learning?" Psychological Review, 9 (1984): 375-391.

Hayashi, Setsuko. Personal Interview. 14 March 1984.

Hearn, Lafcadio. Japan, An Interpretation. New York: Grosset and Dunlap, 1904.

Herrigel, Eugen. Zen and the Art of Archery. London: Routledge and Kegan Paul, 1953.

Kojima, Masami. Personal Interviews. September - December 1983.

Kumagai, Hisa A. "A Dissection of Intimacy: A Study of 'Bi-polar Posturing' in Japanese Social Interaction - "Amaeru" and "Amayakasu" Indulgence and Deference." Culture, Medicine and Psychiatry 5 (1981): 249-272.

Landar, Herbert. Language and Culture. New York: Oxford University Press, 1966.

McDonald, Marjorie. "Transitional Tunes and Musical Development." Psychoanalytic Study of the Child, 25 (1970): 503-521.

Miller, Andrew Roy. Japan's Modern Myth: The Language and Beyond. New York: John Weatherhill, 1982.

Montagu, Ashley. Growing Young. New York: McGraw-Hill, 1981.

Montessori, Maria. The Absorbent Mind. New York: Holt, Rinehart and Weston, 1967.

"Music Rules Inside Everyone's Head." The Daily Yomiuri, 13 September 1983: P. 3.

Nakamura, Hajime. "Consciousness of the Individual and the Universal Among the Japanese." The Japanese Mind: Essentials of Japanese Philosophy and Culture. Edited by Charles A. Moore. Tokyo: Charles E. Tuttle, 1967.

Nakane, Chie. Japanese Society. Tokyo: Charles E. Tuttle, 1970.

Nickels, Carroll. "In Defense of Suzuki." The Strad, October 1974: 273-281.

Nitobe, Inazo. Bushido: The Soul of Japan. Tokyo: Charles E. Tuttle, 1969.

Ono, Susumu. "The Japanese Language: Its Origins and Sources." Japanese Culture. Edited by Robert Smith and Richard Beardsley. Chicago: Aldine Publishing House, 1967.

Piaget, Jean. The Origins of Intelligence in Children. Translated by Margaret Cook. New York: W.W. Norton, 1952.

Piaget, Jean, and Inhelder, Barbel. The Psychology of the Child. Translated by Helen Weaver. New York: Basic Books, 1969.

Pines, Maya. "Baby, You're Incredible." Psychology Today, 16 (1982): 48-53.

Price, Gary Glen. "Mnemonic Support and Curriculum Selection in Teaching by Mothers: A Conjoint Effect." Child Development, 55 (1984): 375-391.

Reilly, Robert R., et al. Educational Psychology. New York: Macmillan, 1983.

Reischauer, Edwin O. The Japanese. Tokyo: Charles E. Tuttle, 1977.

Sapir, Edwin. Language Thought and Culture. Ann Arbor: University of Michigan Press, 1965.

Sarch, Kenneth. "The Suzuki System: A Critical Evaluation." American String Teacher, Summer 1970: 6-11.

Shapiro, Harvey A. "The Japanese Sense of Nature: Where I Found It." Japan Quarterly, 32 (1985): 67-69.

Shimahara, Nobuo K. Adaptation and Education in Japan. New York: Praeger, 1979.

Sibitani, Atuhiro. "The Japanese Brain." Science 80. December 1980: 22-27.

Soseki, Natsume. I Am a Cat (pt. 2). Translated by It., Aido. Tokyo: Charles E. Tuttle, 1979.

Sugishita, Ayako. Personal Interview. 23 February 1984.

"Survey Shows Young People Without Vitality or Objectives." The Japan Times, 13 February 1984: 15.

Suzuki, Daisetsu Teitaro. "An Interpretation of Zen Experience." The Japanese Mind: Essentials of Japanese Philosophy and Culture. Edited by Charles A. Moore. Tokyo: Charles E. Tuttle, 1967.

Suzuki, D.T. Zen and Japanese Culture. New York: Pantheon Books, 1959.

Suzuki, D.T. Zen Buddhism. Edited by William Barrett. USA: Anchor Press. 1956.

Suzuki, Shinichi. Ability Development From Age Zero. Translated Mary Louise Nagata. Secaucus, New Jersey: Summy-Birchard Inc., 1981.

Suzuki, S. Nurtured by Love: A New Approach to Education. Translated by Waltraud Suzuki. Secaucus, New Jersey: Summy-Birchard Inc., 1969.

Suzuki, S. "On Character Formation." Talent Education Journal, 17 (1984): 29-40.

Suzuki, S. "The Law of Ability and The Mother Tongue Method of Education" (Pamphlet). Excerpts from a talk given to the Japan Institute of Educational Psychology, October 16, 1973.

Suzuki, S. "To President Carter and Members of Congress: A Petition for a National Policy For Nurturing Children from Age Zero Years Old" (Pamphlet). 1978.

Suzuki, S. Where Love is Deep. Translated by Kyoko Selden. St. Louis: Talent Education Journal, 1982.

Sweeny, Joan. "Skinner of Education: Kids OK, Methods Aren't." The Japan Times, 9 September 1983: P. 14.

Taniuchi, Lois. Unpublished Doctoral Dissertaion.

Tesshi, Furukawa. "The Individual in Japanese Ethics." The Japanese Mind: Essentials of Japanese Philosophy and Culture. Edited by Charles A. Moore. Tokyo: Charles E. Tuttle, 1967.

Toepfer, Conrad F. "Curriculum Design and Neuropsychological Development." Journal of Research and Development in Education, 15 (1982): 1-11.

Trehub, Sandra E., et al. "Infants' Perception of Melodies: The Role of Melodic Contour." Child Development, 55 (1984): 821-830.

Tucker, Don M., et al. "Asymmetric Neural Control Systems in Human Self-Regulation." Psychological Review, 9 (1984): 185-215.

Wagatsuma, Hiroshi. "Some Cultural Assumptions Among the Japanese." Japan Quarterly, 32 (1984): 371-379.

Walters, R.D. "Some Conditions Facilitating the Occurrence of Imitative Behavior." Social Facilitation and Imitative Behavior. Edited by E.C. Simmel. Boston: Allyn and Bacon, 1968.

Yamagiwa, Joseph K. "Language as an Expression of Japanese Culture." Twelve Doors to Japan. Edited by John W. Hall and R. Richard Beardsley. New York: McGraw-Hill, 1965.